Gao's Music For Olympic Games

Johnson K. Gao

Dallas, Texas, USA

2008

Gao's Music For Olympic Games

http://lulu.com/content/2102738

First published in the United States of America in 2008

By Johnson K. Gao

Dallas, Texas

Cover design and book formatting by Johnson K. Gao

The front cover had used the image of an oil-on-canvas painting –

"A Ballet Girl In A Garden" by Raymond F. Gao with his permission.

First edition, May 2008

ISBN: 978-0-6152-0989-0

To Catherine Gao, my wife,

For her kindness in reminding me not to sit

In front of a computer addictively

To do the work for music creation,

That had hurt my aged eyes, heart and brain, etc.

Fortunately to readers, she had not whipped me away

From my desk for tedious or even painful work -

By inputting thousands of music notes

For song composition,

So as not to prevent me totally from

Completion of those music CDs and

This pamphlet of music sheets and lyrics

For the Olympic Games and other events.

Contents

Olympic Marching Song

Original Chinese lyrics by Johnson Gao
English translation by Catherine Gao

Johnson Gao

Allegro

Soprano / Tenor lyrics:

Ao lin— pi ke, Ao lin— pi ke, yi qi feng fa. la la la la la la la la la la
O- lym - pic, O- lym- pic, s - pi - rits high. la la la la la la la la la la

la la la la. Ao lin pi ke, Ao lin pi ke, jie bao fei yang. la la la la la
la la la la. O- lym- pic, O- lym- pic, new re - cords fly. la la la la la

la la la la la la la la la.   Wu zhou jian   er, huan ying___ nin!   Ge guo
la la la la la la la la la.   Good ath - le - tes, we wel - come you!   No - ble

gui bin, huan ying____ nin! Shi jie__ ren min xiang ju__ yi qi gong__ huan__
gue - sts, we wel - come you! Fi - ve__ conti - nen - tal__ people are in great

28
S.
T.
A.
B.
Picc. Tpt.
Cnt.
Dr.
Cym.
le. Ao lin pi ke you yi zhi guang wan nian chang qing!
joy. Tor-ch of friend- ship burns for - e - ver!

奥林匹克 进行曲

高魁雄词

（为２００８北京奥林匹克运动会而作）

奥林匹克，奥林匹克，

意气风发。

啦啦啦啦啦，

啦啦啦啦啦 - 啦啦啦啦。

奥林匹克，奥林匹克，

捷报飞扬。

啦啦啦啦啦，

啦啦啦啦啦 - 啦啦啦啦。

五洲健儿，欢迎您！

各国贵宾，欢迎您！

五洲健儿，欢迎您！

各国贵宾，欢迎您！

世界人民相聚一起共欢乐。

奥林匹克友谊之光万年长青!

"Olympic Marching Song"

For 2008 Olympic Games in Beijing (in Mandarin Pinyin)

Ao-lin-pi-ke, Ao-lin-pi-ke,
Yiqi fengfa.
Lalalalala-
Lalalalala-lalala.
Ao-lin-pi-ke, Ao-lin-pi-ke,
Jiebao feiying.
Lalalalala-
Lalalalala-lalala.
Wuzhou jian-er, huanying nin!
Geguo guibin, huanying nin!
Wuzhou jian-er, huanying nin!
Geguo guibin, huanying nin!
Shijie renmin xiangju yiqi gong huanle.
Ao-lin-pi-ke youyi zhiguang wannian changqing!

Johnson Gao

(For 2008 Olympic Games in Beijing)

Translated in English

from the original lyrics in Chinese written by

Johnson Gao

Olympic Marching Song

Olympic, Olympic,

Spirits high.

Lalalalala,

Lalalalala-lalalala.

Olympic, Olympic,

New records fly.

Lalalalala,

Lalalalala-lalalala.

Good athletes, we welcome you!

Noble guests, we welcome you!

Good athletes, we welcome you!

Noble guests, we welcome you!

Five continental people are in great joy!

Torch of friendship burns forever!

Song For Success

Johnson Gao

Johnson Gao

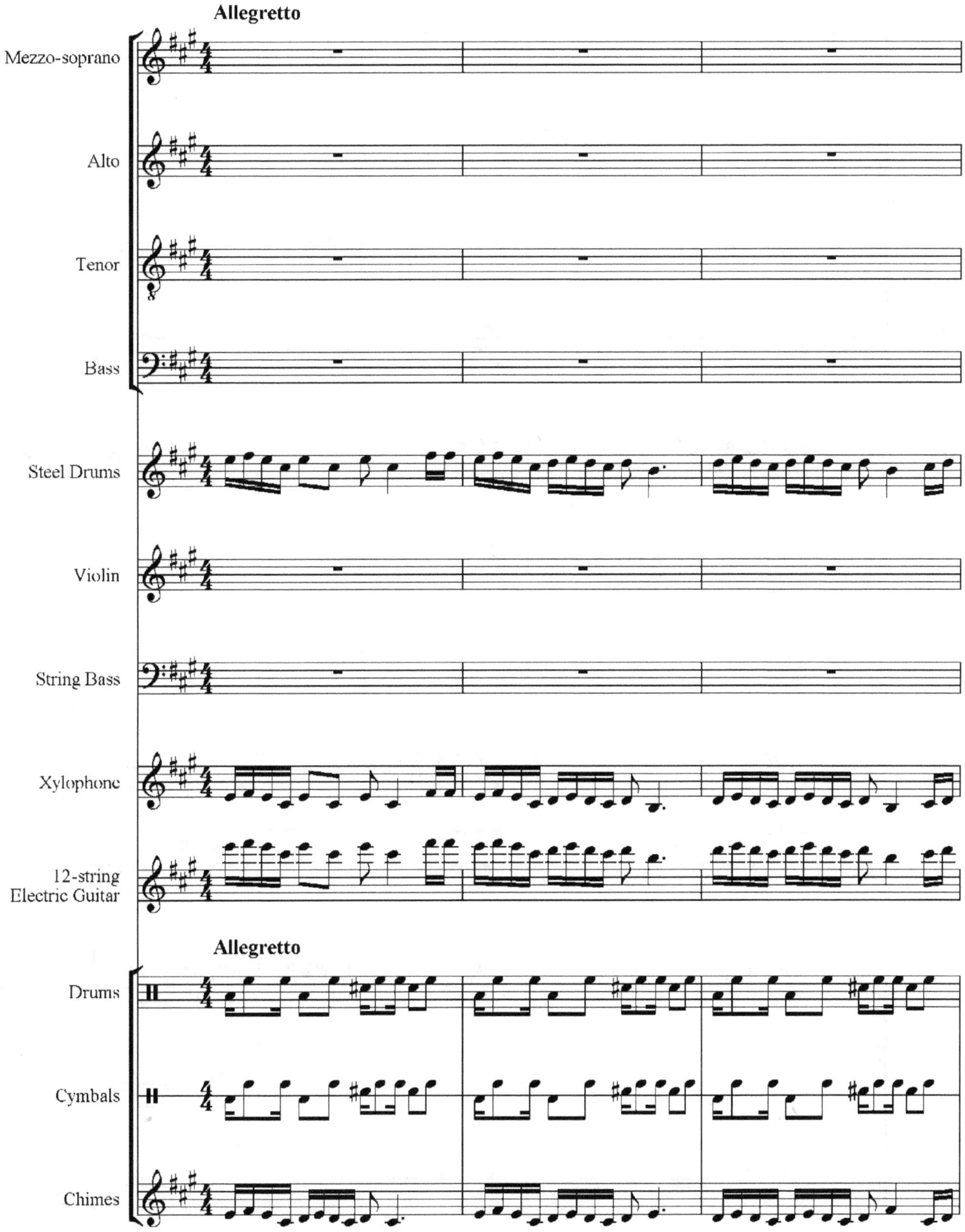

2

Bei-jing Olym - pic Games

11

7
M-S.
are ve - ry won der- ful. Ve- ry,
A.
T.
B.
Steel D.
Vln.
S. Bass
Xyl.
E. Gtr.
Dr.
Cym.
Chim.

4

ve - ry___ wonder ful._____ "Tis suc cess ful._____

Bei jing is_ in_ joy._

We are

15
M-S.
hal - le - luah,
Ah! Ah! Ah!
A.
T.
B.
Steel D.
Vln.
S. Bass
Xyl.
E. Gtr.
Dr.
Cym.
Chim.

18
M-S.
We are hal - le- luah.
We are
A.
T.
B.
Steel D.
Vln.
S. Bass
Xyl.
E. Gtr.
Dr.
Cym.
Chim.

hal - le- luah._____ We are hal- le- luah._____

Go - od_ath - le - tes   cre - ated   those new___ re - cords.

O - re__ no - ble__gue - sts   bro - ght__ in__frie   nd - shi -p.   We use our smiles to

30
M-S.
sa - lute s-ports' he - roes. We use our faithes to build a common goal.
A.
T.
B.
Steel D.
Vln.
S. Bass
Xyl.
E. Gtr.
Dr.
Cym.
Chim.

12

For___ Citius,___ Altius,___ Fortius___ we're marching on.

21

Torch of_ Olym - pic_ burns__ bright and long.

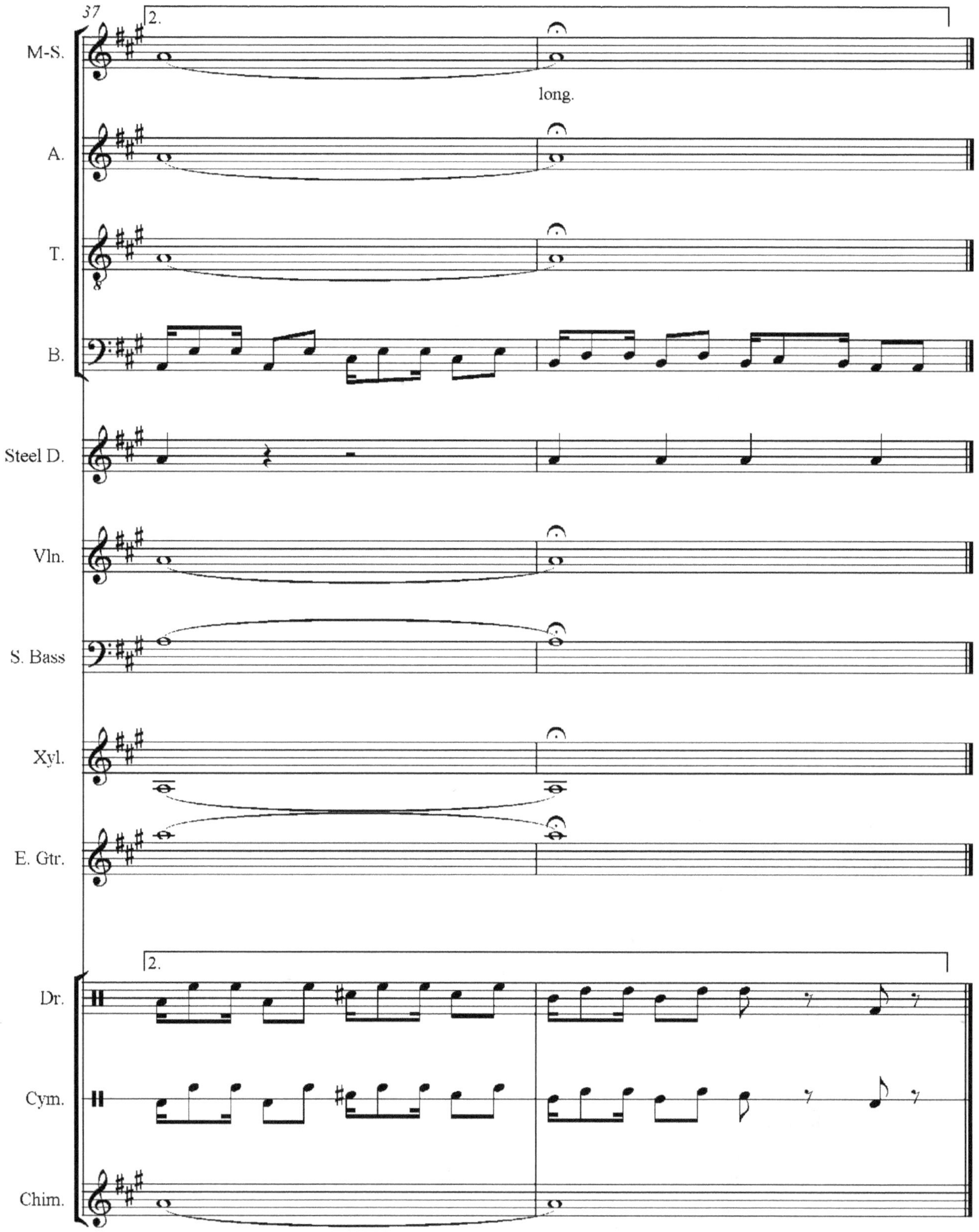
37
2.
M-S.
long.
A.
T.
B.
Steel D.
Vln.
S. Bass
Xyl.
E. Gtr.
2.
Dr.
Cym.
Chim.

Beijing Opera Style Olympic Song

Johnson Gao

Johnson Gao

24

Ao Yun Hui kai_____ mu liao_____ Bei - jing_____
shi____ fen xian_____ dai hua._____ Gu____ cheng_____

xian de zhen___ re_____ nao._____ Xian hua gun gun ru___ hai lang___
ying zi tian___ xin_____ mao._____ Wei le geng kui geng gao, geng___ jian zhuang,

Jin qi hua hua dao chu piao.____ Dao chu piao.____ Dao____ chu
wu zhou____ jian_____ er_____ cheng ying hao.____ Cheng ying

28
S.
A.
T.
piao. Dao ya mo dao chu piao.
hao. Cheng ya mocheng ying hao.
B.
Choir
Vln. 1
Vln. II
S. Bass
H. S. Gtr.
Chim.
Dr.
Cym.

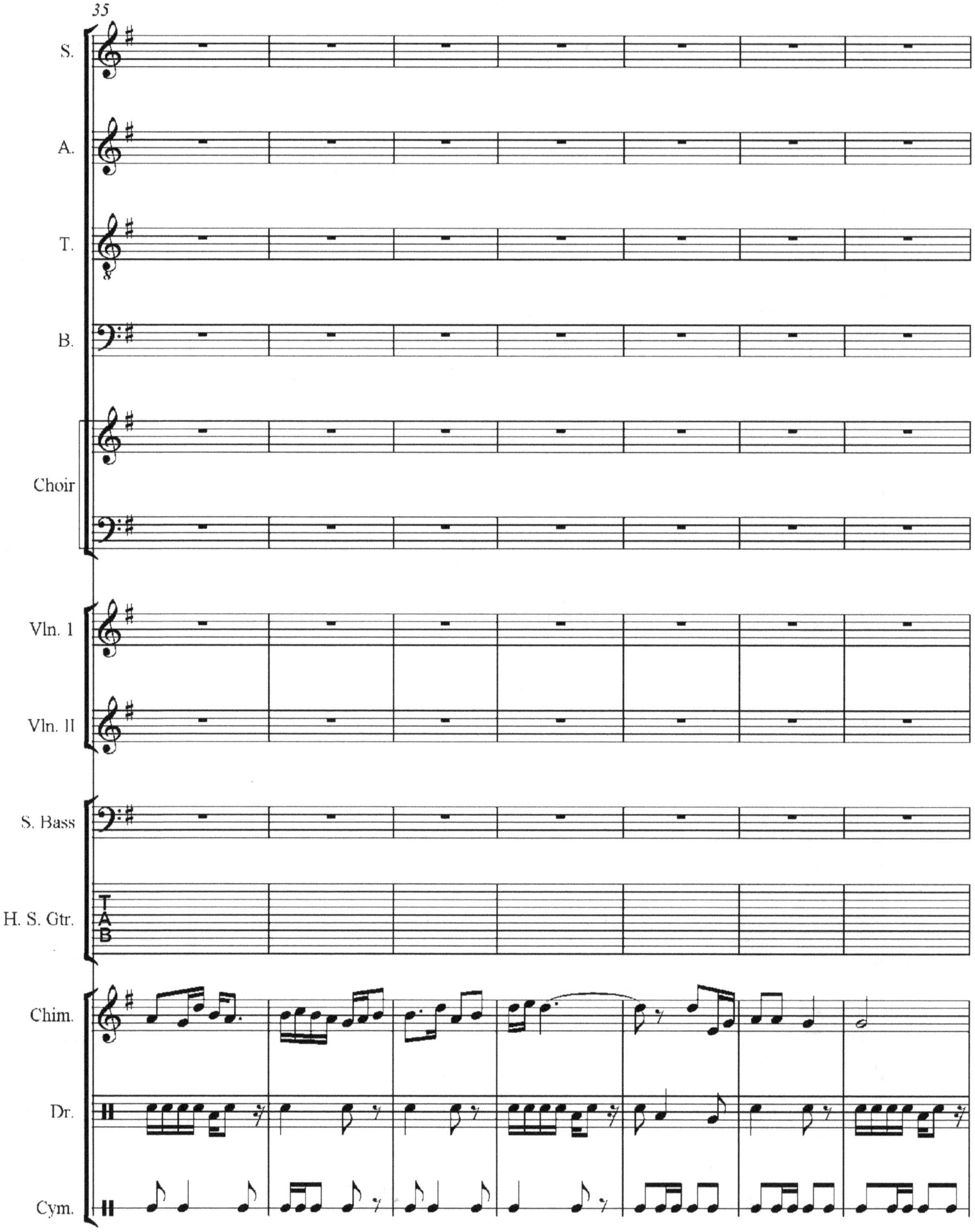
35
S.
A.
T.
B.
Choir
Vln. 1
Vln. II
S. Bass
H. S. Gtr.
Chim.
Dr.
Cym.

42
S.
A.
T.
(1)Sai chang hao bi
(2)Ao Yun huo ju
B.
Choir
Vln. 1
Vln. II
S. Bass
H. S. Gtr.
Chim.
Dr.
Cym.

8

yi___ zuo   you___ yi___ jin   qiao._____ A!_____
xiong_ xiong   zai_____ ran   shao._____ A!_____

55
S.
A.
T.
A!_____ You yi jin_ qiao. A!___ A!_ A!___ A!___ Jie bao pin chuan wu zhou si hai
A!_____ Zai ran_____ shao. A!___ A!_ A!___ A!___ He ping zhi guang ren lei qi wang
B.
Choir
Vln. 1
Vln. II
S. Bass
H. S. Gtr.
Chim.
Dr.
Cym.

zai huan xiao. Ji yi mei de jiao liu ji hui hao.
he xu yao. Ping deng hu li ren ren ai.

Ji___ hui___ hao_____ Zhen ya mozhen zhen hao._____
Lyu__ se___ huan bao_____ wei hou dai ba fu zao._____

12

35

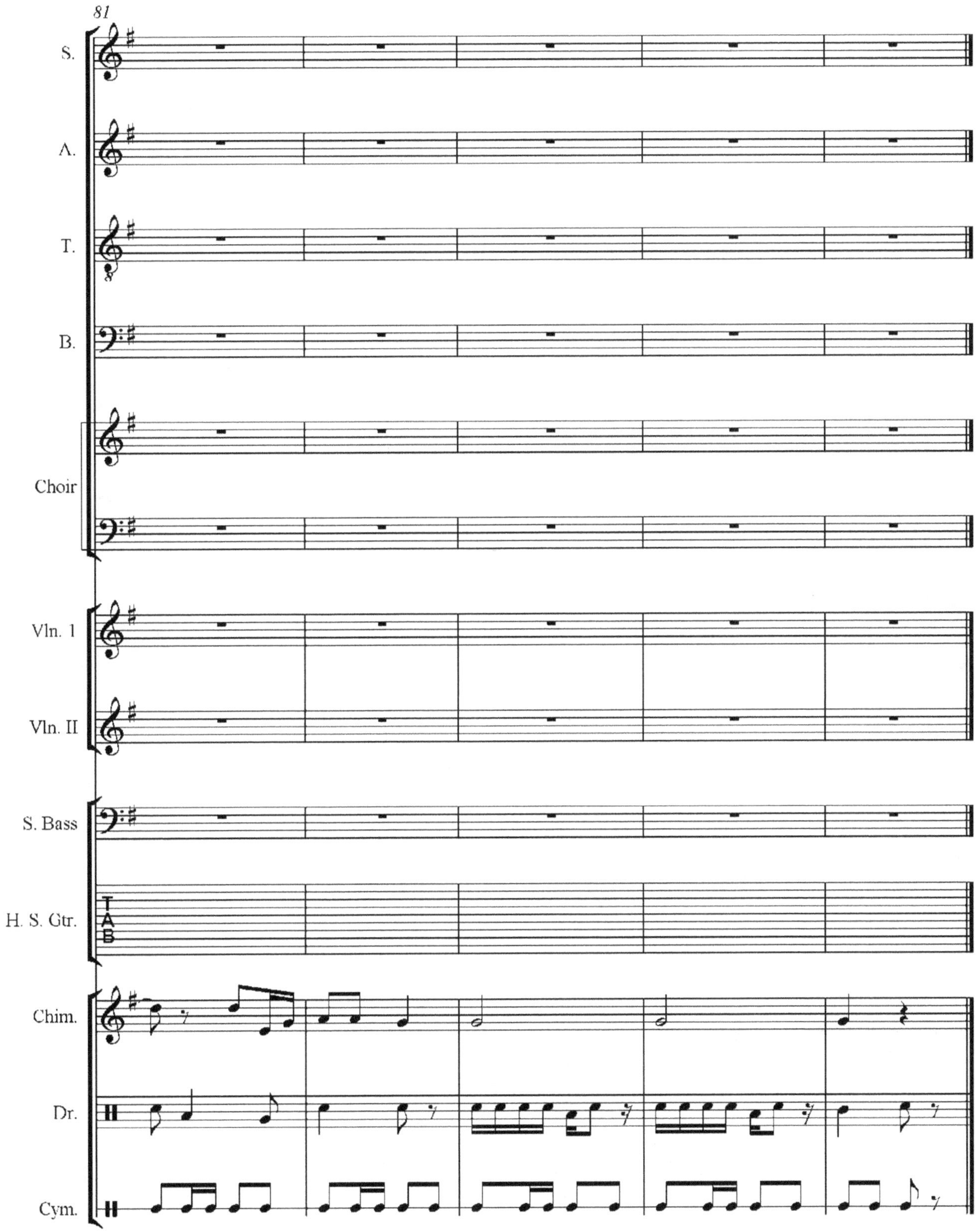
81
S.
A.
T.
B.
Choir
Vln. 1
Vln. II
S. Bass
H. S. Gtr.
TAB
Chim.
Dr.
Cym.

京剧式奥运会歌 高魁雄作词

二十九届奥运会开幕了。

北京显得真热闹。

鲜花滚滚如海浪。

锦旗哗哗到处飘。

到处飘，到处飘，到呀么到处飘。

场馆设施十分现代化。

古城英姿添新貌。

为了更快，更高，更健壮，

五洲健儿逞英豪。

逞英豪，逞英豪，逞呀么逞英豪。

赛场好比一座友谊金桥。

啊！啊！友谊金桥。啊！啊！啊！啊！

捷报频传，五洲四海在欢笑。

技艺美德交流机会好。

机会好，真呀么真真好。

奥运火炬熊熊在燃烧。

啊！啊！在燃烧。啊！啊！啊！啊！

和平之光人类期望和需要。

平等互利人人爱。

绿色环保为后代把福造。

Olympic Is Good (in Chinese and English)

Johnson Gao

Johnson Gao

Soprano:
Ao lin pi ke jiu shi hao.
(Bei jing) re qing huan ying nin! __
(jiu shi hao, jiu shi hao, jiu shi hao,) Huoju
(huan ying nin, huanying nin, huanying nin,) Shi jie

2

xiongxiong zai ran shao.　　(zai　ran shao, zai　ran shao,　zai　ran shao,)　WuZou jian er　xi xiang

ren　min gong huan xiao.　(gong huan xiao, gong huan xiao,　gong huan xiao,)　You yi　zhi hua yong bu

11
S.
feng, (xi xiang feng, xi xiang feng, xi xiang feng,) Shua xin ji lu pan xin
xie, (yong bu xie, yong bu xie, yong bu xie,) He ping fan rong xian lang
T.
A.
B.
Bagp.
Steel D.
E Hn.
Br.
Dr.
Cym.

4

S.: gao. (pan xin gao, pan xin gao, pan xin gao,) Bei jing is___ go___
chao. (xian lang chao, xian lang chao, xina lang chao,) Olym pic come you to Bei

41

Light torch is burn ing.
World peo ple are halleluiah!

6

(burning,___ burning, burning,) Ath le tes are in joy. (joy,___ joy,___
(halleluiah! halleluiah! halleluiah!) Friend ship will never die. (never die, never die,

43

S.

joy,)___ Raise re or__ ds to the new_ height. (heights,__ heights,__
never_ die,) Push pie_ ce_ to a new_ tide.

T.

A.

B.

Bagp.

Steel D.

E Hn.

Br.

Dr.

Cym.

heights,)_ WeL

(a new tide, a new tide, a new tide.)

Raise the Championship Cup - Ju Guanjun Bei

Johnson Gao

Johnson Gao

2

shou jiang tai, ju jin___ bei, wu shang guang rong. Zhe shi

on the deck. Raise championship cup__ That's a glo - ry. It is

47

10
S.
A.
sheng li de xiang zheng. Zhe shi pin bo de jie
T.
Choir
a sign of vic tory. It is a crystal of
H-t. Pno.
E Hn.
E. Gtr.
TAB

4

jing,_____ jian chi de cheng guo._____ ku le de jiao rong._____

stru - gle._____ a fruit of efforts. _____ Mix bitter with_ joy. _____

49

19
S.
A.
Dan wo qing chu zhi dao, wo bu neng yong yuan ting liu zai
T.
Choir
But, it is clear to me. I shouldn't stop here for
H-t. Pno.
E Hn.
E. Gtr.

6

Lyrics under Alto staff: yuan chu. Wo bi xi ji xu nu li, jia bei de nu____ li.____

Lyrics under Choir staff: e - ver. I have to be going on. I have to be going on.

51

28
S.
A.
Zai ying xiong hou mian you xu duo ying xiong. A! Ren lei de zhi___ hui,
T.
Choir
There are heroes___ behind one hero.___ A! For our___ human___ being,
H-t. Pno.
E Hn.
E. Gtr.
T
A
B

32
S.
A.
ren lei de neng li, ren lei de pan deng wu qiong.
T.
Choir
there is no boun - da - ry as for our wis - dom, ability, or, clibing!
H-t. Pno.
E Hn.
E. Gtr.
T
A
B

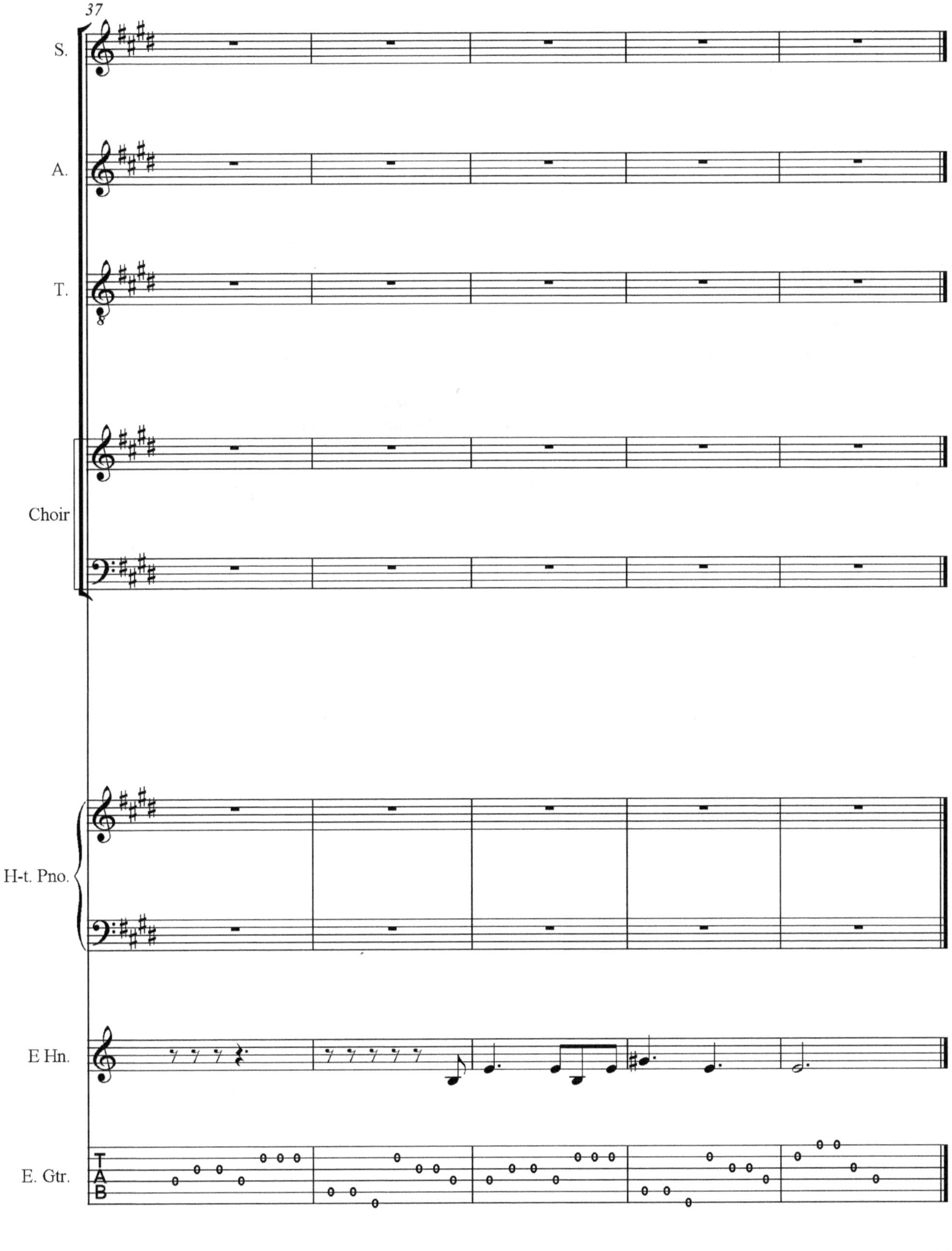
37
S.
A.
T.
Choir
H-t. Pno.
E Hn.
E. Gtr.
T
A
B

Name: Johnson Gao

Class _____

For Mammy

Mammy,   Mammy,   I   love   you.   Mammy,   Mammy,   I   love   you.
Mammy,   Mammy,   I   love   you.   Mammy,   Mammy,   I   love   you.

You   are   caring.   You   are   kind.   You brought me to the   beautiful   world.
You   are   smiling   in   my   heart.   Happy'n   healthy   I   wish   you.

For Daddy

Daddy, Daddy, I love you.
I wish you happy!
You taught me how to learn and how to play.
Knowledge and science increase my power.
You led me be friend with all of them.

Daddy, Daddy, I love you.
I wish you healthy!
You taught me how to swim and how to paint.
Swim in the pool and swim in real life.
Paint a rainbow and paint every colorful day.

Johnson Gao

獻給爸爸　　　高魁雄詞

爸爸，爸爸，我愛您。我祝您愉快。

您教我怎樣學習，怎樣遊玩。

科學和知識增加我力量。

您引導我與它們成為朋友。

爸爸，爸爸，我愛您。我祝您健康。

您教我游泳，教我把圖繪。

游在泳池里，游在生活中。

畫道彩虹，畫得明天更光輝。

For Dad

Johnson Gao

Johnson Gao

Dad- dy, Dad - dy, I love you. I wish you hap - py.
Dad- dy, Dad - dy, I love you. I wish you heal - thy.

You taught me - how to learn and how to play. Science and know-le-
You taught me - how to swim and hwo to paint. swim in the po-

dge increase my pow - er. You taught me be friends with all of them.
-ol, swim in the li - fe. Piant a rain bow and every coler - ful day.

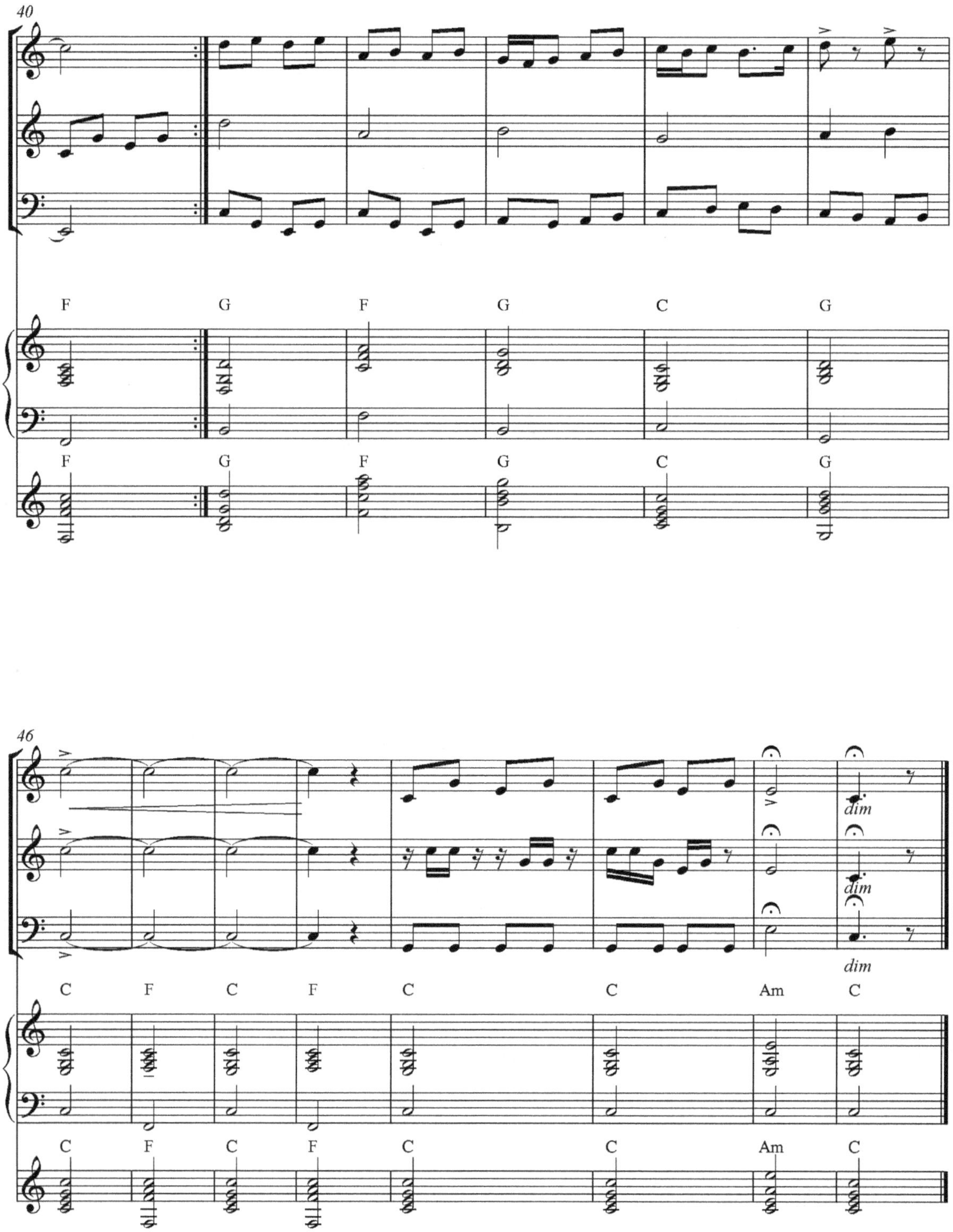
40
F
G
F
G
C
G
F
G
F
G
C
G
46
dim
dim
dim
C
F
C
F
C
C
Am
C
C
F
C
F
C
C
Am
C

The Snow

Johnson K. Gao

The Tenor voice of this music was composed arround 1966 for the poem "The Snow" by Mao Zedong in 1936. Lyrics in Pinyin under the Tenor.

60

2

The Tenor voice of this music was composed arround 1966 for the poem "The Snow" by Mao Zedong in 1936. Lyrics in Pinyin under the Tenor.

61

The Tenor voice of this music was composed arround 1966 for the poem "The Snow" by Mao Zedong in 1936. Lyrics in Pinyin under the Tenor.

Beiguo feng   guang,

qian - li bing feng,   wan li xue piao.

The Tenor voice of this music was composed arround 1966 for the poem "The Snow" by Mao Zedong in 1936. Lyrics in Pinyin under the Tenor.

The Tenor voice of this music was composed arround 1966 for the poem "The Snow" by Mao Zedong in 1936. Lyrics in Pinyin under the Tenor.

da he___ shang xia, dun shi___ tao___ tao.

Shan wu ying she,yuan shi la_xiang, yu_ yu_ tian gong

The Tenor voice of this music was composed arround 1966 for the poem "The Snow" by Mao Zedong in 1936. Lyrics in Pinyin under the Tenor.

The Tenor voice of this music was composed arround 1966 for the poem "The Snow" by Mao Zedong in 1936. Lyrics in Pinyin under the Tenor.

8

The Tenor voice of this music was composed arround 1966 for the poem "The Snow" by Mao Zedong in 1936. Lyrics in Pinyin under the Tenor.

The Tenor voice of this music was composed arround 1966 for the poem "The Snow" by Mao Zedong in 1936. Lyrics in Pinyin under the Tenor.

10

The Tenor voice of this music was composed arround 1966 for the poem "The Snow" by Mao Zedong in 1936. Lyrics in Pinyin under the Tenor.

69

The Tenor voice of this music was composed arround 1966 for the poem "The Snow" by Mao Zedong in 1936. Lyrics in Pinyin under the Tenor.

12

The Tenor voice of this music was composed arround 1966 for the poem "The Snow" by Mao Zedong in 1936. Lyrics in Pinyin under the Tenor.

71

hai   kanjin_____   zhao.

The Tenor voice of this music was composed arround 1966 for the poem "The Snow" by Mao Zedong in 1936. Lyrics in Pinyin under the Tenor.

The Tenor voice of this music was composed arround 1966 for the poem "The Snow" by Mao Zedong in 1936. Lyrics in Pinyin under the Tenor.

The Six Plate-shaped Mountains

Mao Zeding

Johnson K. Gao

1. Lyrics was added under the Tenor voice. and Alto and Bass are similar to the Tenor.
2. Sections 12-31 of the Alto and Bass song "Ah" word, and sections 35-50 of Saprano songs "Ah!" word also.

1. Lyrics was added under the Tenor voice, and Alto and Bass are similar to the Tenor.
2. Sections 12-31 of the Alto and Bass song "Ah" word, and sections 35-50 of Saprano songs "Ah!" word also.

1. Lyrics was added under the Tenor voice, and Alto and Bass are similar to the Tenor.
2. Sections 12-31 of the Alto and Bass song "Ah" word, and sections 35-50 of Saprano songs "Ah!" word also.

1. Lyrics was added under the Tenor voice, and Alto and Bass are similar to the Tenor.
2. Sections 12-31 of the Alto and Bass song "Ah" word, and sections 35-50 of Saprano songs "Ah!" word also.

1. Lyrics was added under the Tenor voice, and Alto and Bass are similar to the Tenor.
2. Sections 12-31 of the Alto and Bass song "Ah" word, and sections 35-50 of Saprano songs "Ah!" word also.

1. Lyrics was added under the Tenor voice, and Alto and Bass are similar to the Tenor.
2. Sections 12-31 of the Alto and Bass song "Ah" word, and sections 35-50 of Saprano songs "Ah!" word also.

1. Lyrics was added under the Tenor voice, and Alto and Bass are similar to the Tenor.
2. Sections 12-31 of the Alto and Bass song "Ah" word, and sections 35-50 of Saprano songs "Ah!" word also.

1. Lyrics was added under the Tenor voice, and Alto and Bass are similar to the Tenor.
2. Sections 12-31 of the Alto and Bass song "Ah" word, and sections 35-50 of Saprano songs "Ah!" word also.

1. Lyrics was added under the Tenor voice, and Alto and Bass are similar to the Tenor.
2. Sections 12-31 of the Alto and Bass song "Ah" word, and sections 35-50 of Saprano songs "Ah!" word also.

wang   duan nan   fei_____ yian.

1. Lyrics was added under the Tenor voice, and Alto and Bass are similar to the Tenor.
2. Sections 12-31 of the Alto and Bass song "Ah" word, and sections 35-50 of Saprano songs "Ah!" word also.

83

Bu dao chang cheng fei__ hao_ han, qu zhi xing cheng

1. Lyrics was added under the Tenor voice, and Alto and Bass are similar to the Tenor.
2. Sections 12-31 of the Alto and Bass song "Ah" word, and sections 35-50 of Saprano songs "Ah!" word also.

1. Lyrics was added under the Tenor voice, and Alto and Bass are similar to the Tenor.
2. Sections 12-31 of the Alto and Bass song "Ah" word, and sections 35-50 of Saprano songs "Ah!" word also.

gao feng, hong qi man juan xi feng. Jin ri chang ying zai shou, he_____

1. Lyrics was added under the Tenor voice, and Alto and Bass are similar to the Tenor.
2. Sections 12-31 of the Alto and Bass song "Ah" word, and sections 35-50 of Saprano songs "Ah!" word also.

14

1. Lyrics was added under the Tenor voice, and Alto and Bass are similar to the Tenor.
2. Sections 12-31 of the Alto and Bass song "Ah" word, and sections 35-50 of Saprano songs "Ah!" word also.

1. Lyrics was added under the Tenor voice, and Alto and Bass are similar to the Tenor.
2. Sections 12-31 of the Alto and Bass song "Ah" word, and sections 35-50 of Saprano songs "Ah!" word also.

16

1. Lyrics was added under the Tenor voice, and Alto and Bass are similar to the Tenor.
2. Sections 12-31 of the Alto and Bass song "Ah" word, and sections 35-50 of Saprano songs "Ah!" word also.

1. Lyrics was added under the Tenor voice, and Alto and Bass are similar to the Tenor.
2. Sections 12-31 of the Alto and Bass song "Ah" word, and sections 35-50 of Saprano songs "Ah!" word also.

1. Lyrics was added under the Tenor voice, and Alto and Bass are similar to the Tenor.
2. Sections 12-31 of the Alto and Bass song "Ah" word, and sections 35-50 of Saprano songs "Ah!" word also.

A note to three songs

The following pages of music sheet are for three songs that I composed recently. "Become A Peace Locomotor" and "The Endless Joy (For Lion Dance")" were based on the main melodies of two songs that I had composed about fifty years ago, around the year 1957, when I was a high school student in Shanghai, China, after selfstudying the thick book for teaching music composition called as "He Sheng Yu Dui Wei" written by Ding Shan-de. That was happened just before my entering into the Nanjing University (or, the old English name Nanking University) which directed my career to become a developmental biologist and cell biologist. Thus, my life was more involved in science and technology. Thereafter, I was invited as a research professor by three American universities consecutively and finally that led my name to be listed in "American Men and Women of Science". I shall express deep thank to my good memory that I still can recall all of those music notes very clearly after 50 years. Of course, I shall also appreciat the elapse of time that brought in the advanced music softwares to world which enalbled me to use them on an ordingnary set of PC to create, or, to convert the originally simple form of those songs to the current versions with more complicated voices and structures and that let me become not only the music composer but also a "conductor" of a band with verieties of music instrument to perform those songs by myself.

The third song is called as "Bon Voyage! Olympic Games' Athletes!", which is expacted to be used at the closing celemony of Olympic Games. The music alone can be used in any cercumstsnces when one wants to say farewell to his/her friends.

The first two pieces of music had also been added to my newly released CD entitled as "Gao's Music for Olympic Games" that I had published at http://lulu.com. and http://cdbaby.com/cd/johnsongao3. I hope that you will like this music sheet albom and songs in my CD.

Become A Peace Locomotor

Johnson K. Gao

Johnson K. Gao

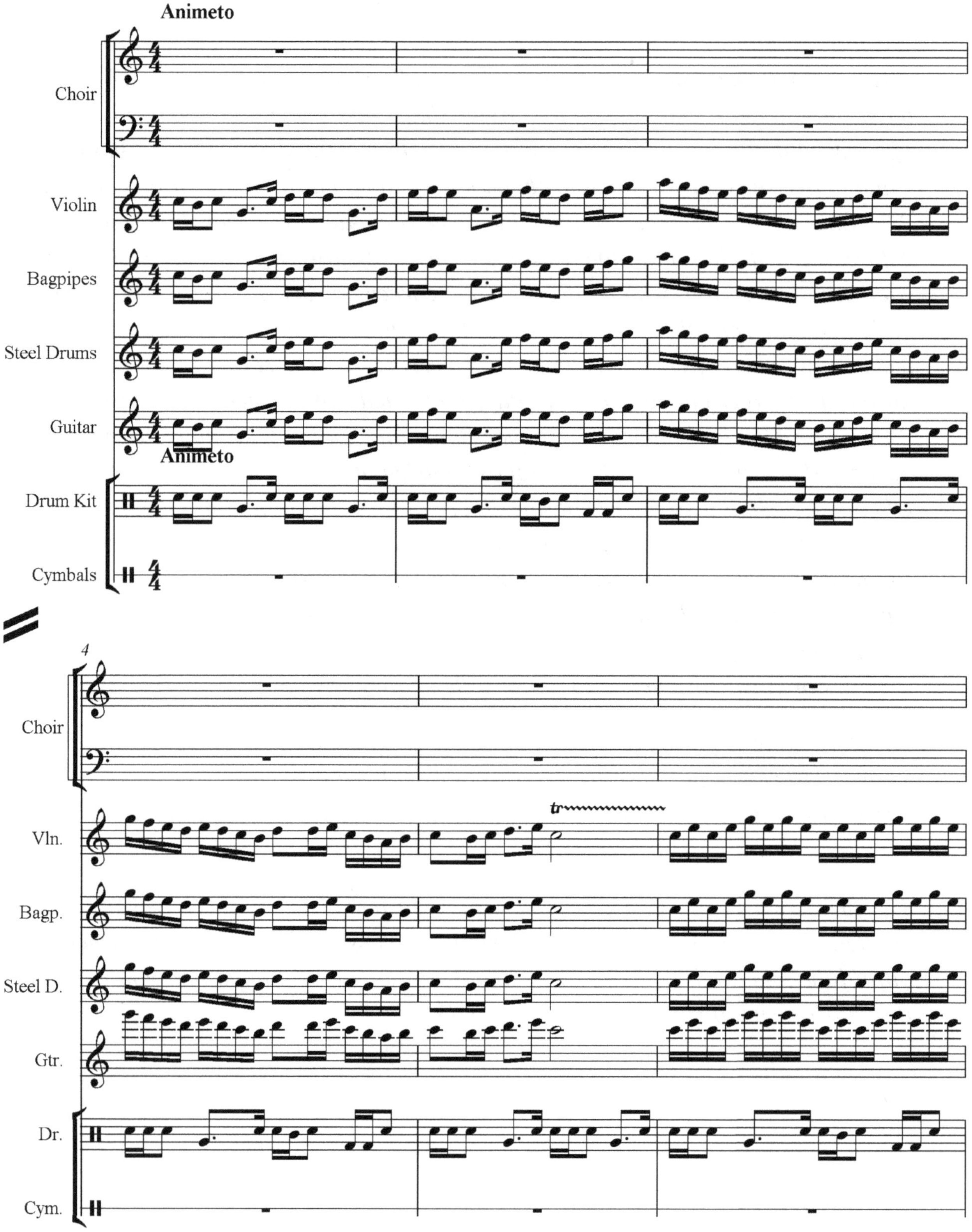

7
Choir
Vln.
Bagp.
Steel D.
Gtr.
Dr.
Cym.
tr
10
Choir
8va
Vln.
Bagp.
Steel D.
Gtr.
Dr.
Cym.
tr

Choir: Olym- pic Games, what's people like. All athletes come from the world.

Choir: For ci-ti-us, for al-ti-us and for for-ti-us we get to-ge-ther. We're hea - lth

4

va - lue than a gold__ me da -

6

35
Choir
Become(a) peace lo-co - motor.
Vln.
Bagp.
(8)
Steel D.
Gtr.
Dr.
Cym.
38
Choir
Become(a) green pro - motor. May our Olym - pic
Vln.
Bagp.
(8)
Steel D.
Gtr.
Dr.
Cym.

8

100

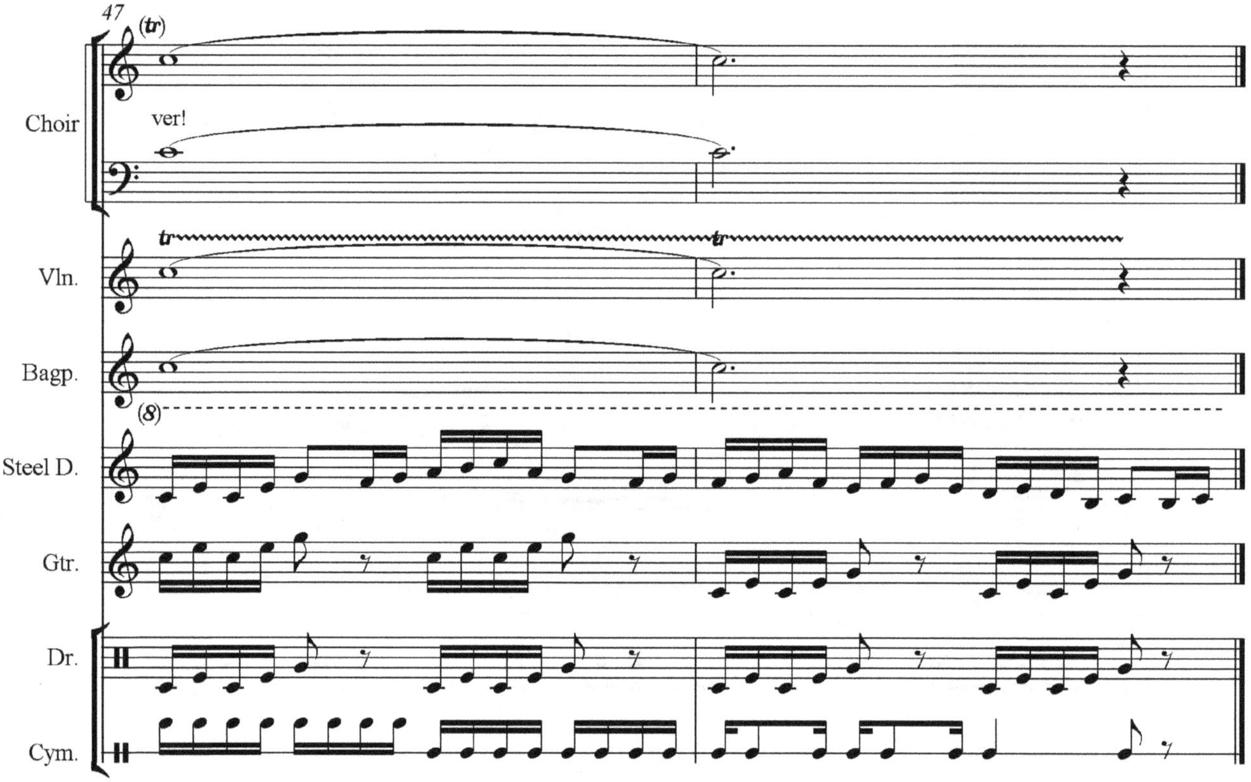
47
(tr)
Choir
ver!
Vln.
tr
Bagp.
(8)
Steel D.
Gtr.
Dr.
Cym.

Endless Joy (Semi-Lion Dance)

Johnson Gao

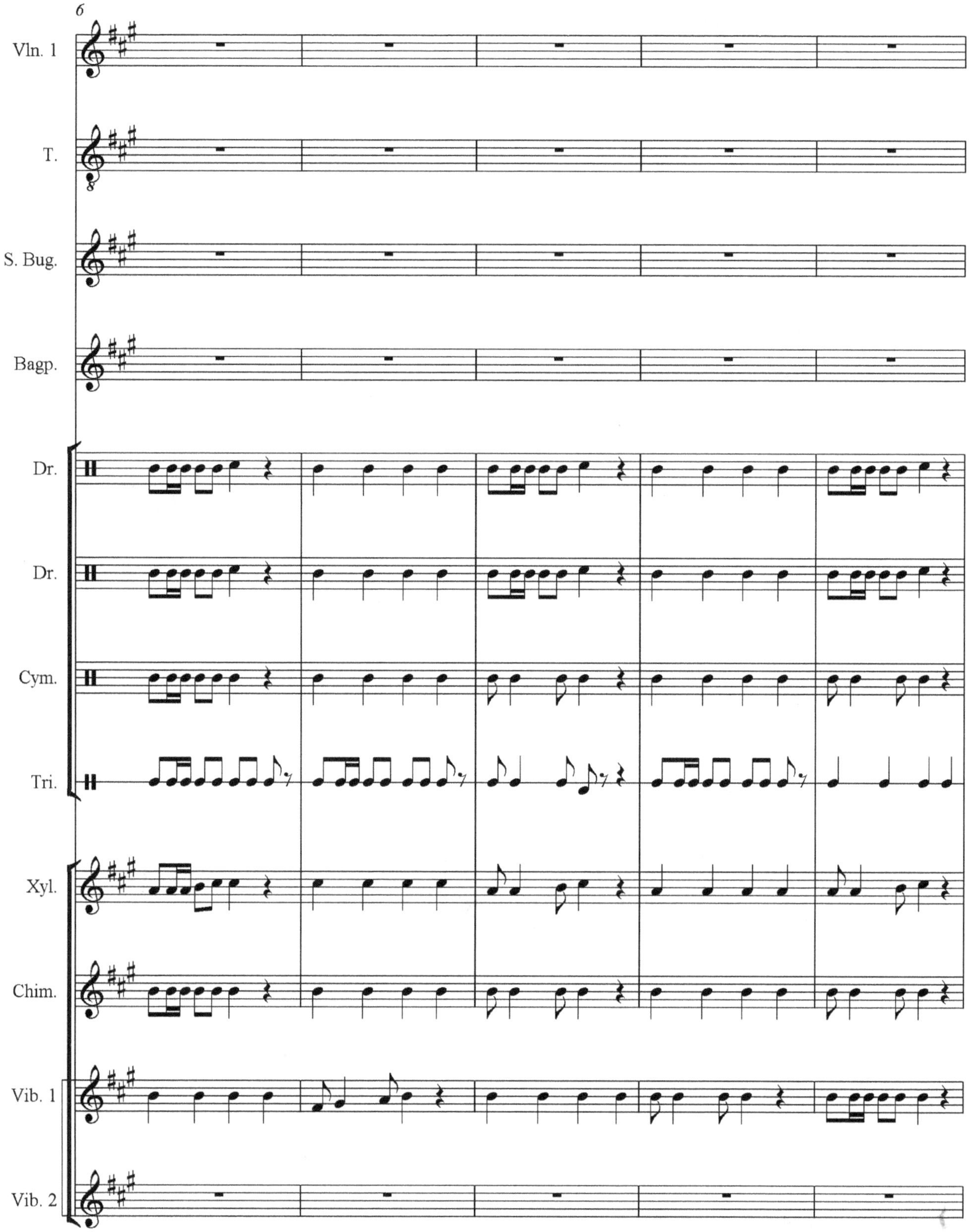
6
Vln. 1
T.
S. Bug.
Bagp.
Dr.
Dr.
Cym.
Tri.
Xyl.
Chim.
Vib. 1
Vib. 2

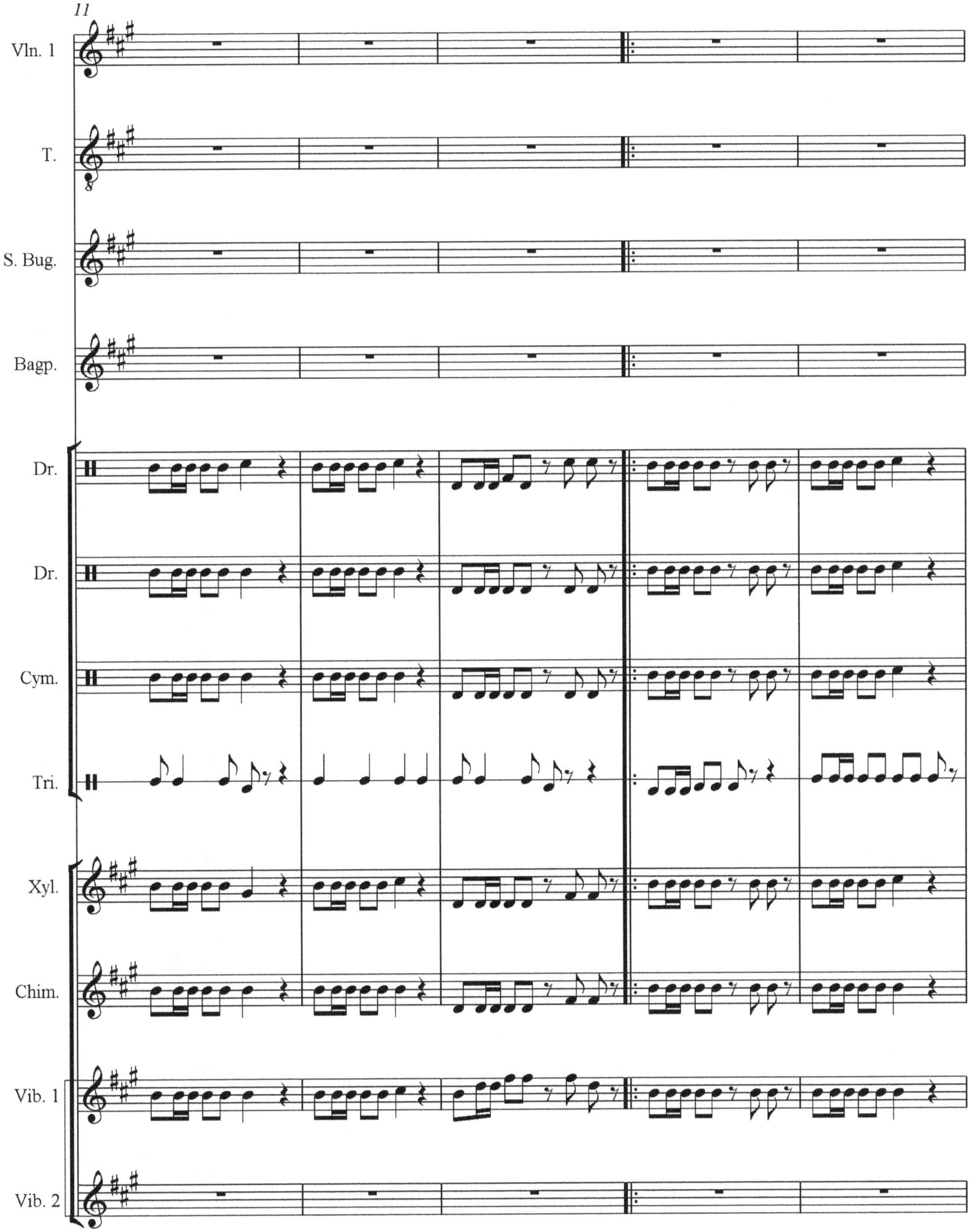
11
Vln. 1
T.
S. Bug.
Bagp.
Dr.
Dr.
Cym.
Tri.
Xyl.
Chim.
Vib. 1
Vib. 2

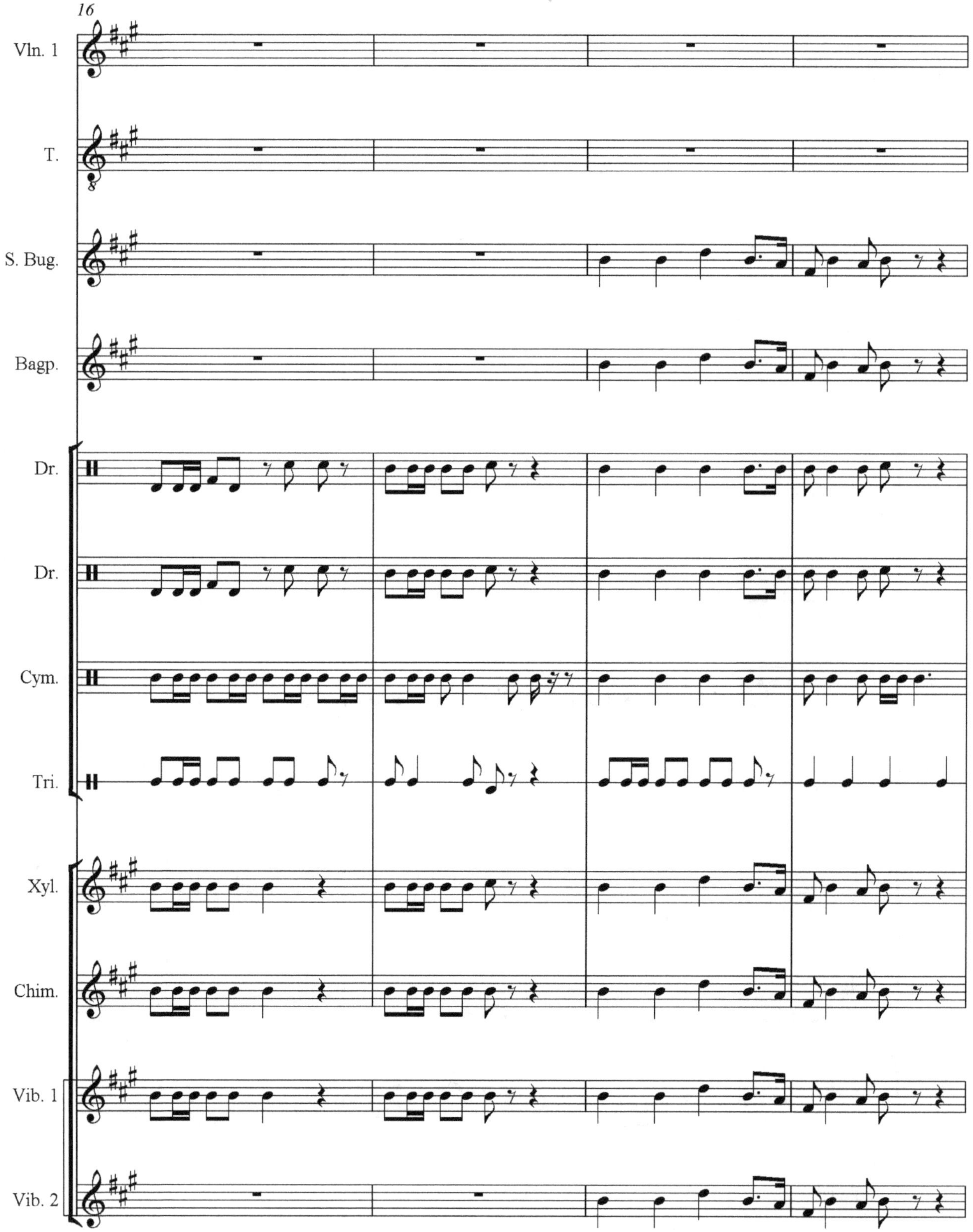
16
Vln. 1
T.
S. Bug.
Bagp.
Dr.
Dr.
Cym.
Tri.
Xyl.
Chim.
Vib. 1
Vib. 2

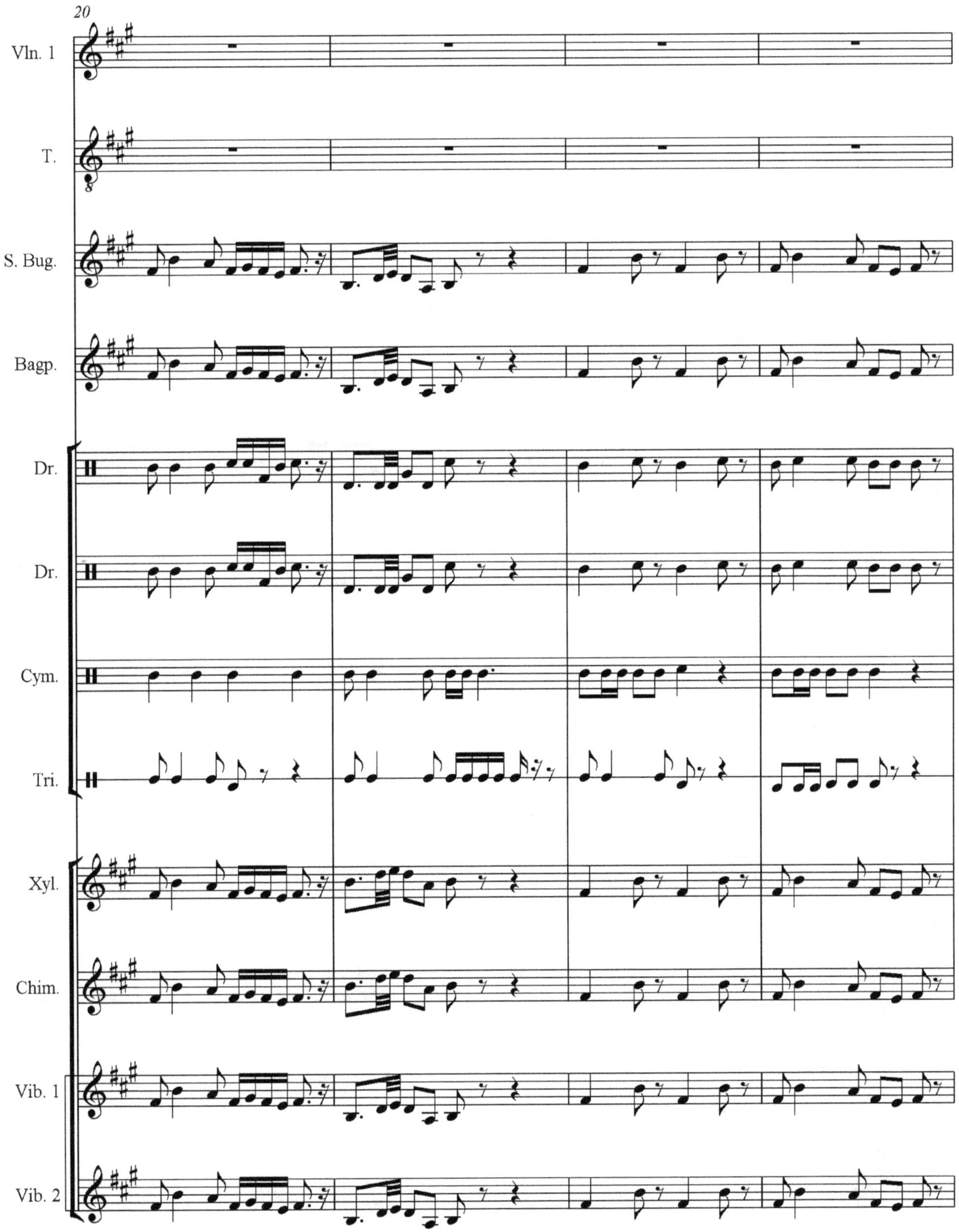
20
Vln. 1
T.
S. Bug.
Bagp.
Dr.
Dr.
Cym.
Tri.
Xyl.
Chim.
Vib. 1
Vib. 2

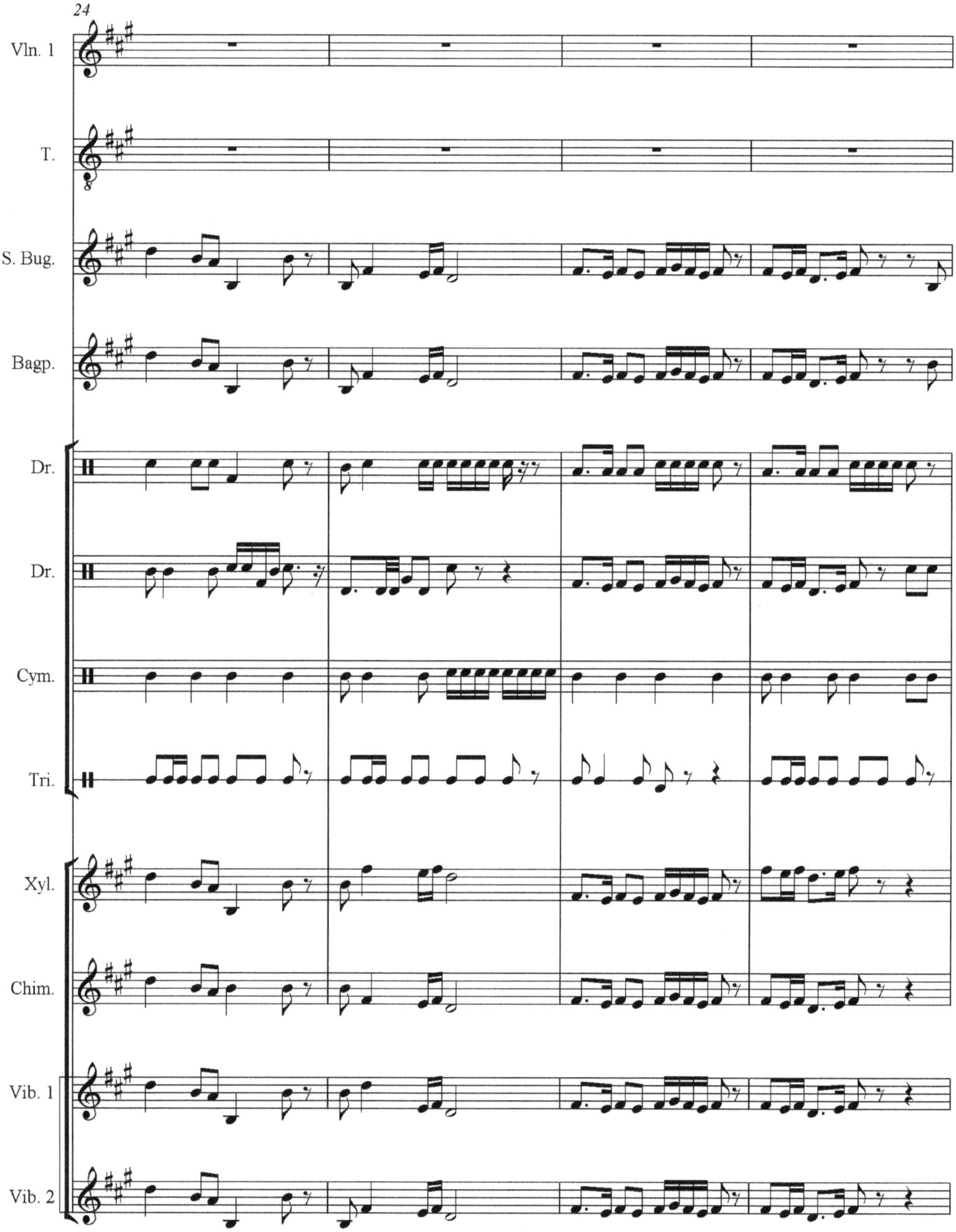
24
Vln. 1
T.
S. Bug.
Bagp.
Dr.
Dr.
Cym.
Tri.
Xyl.
Chim.
Vib. 1
Vib. 2

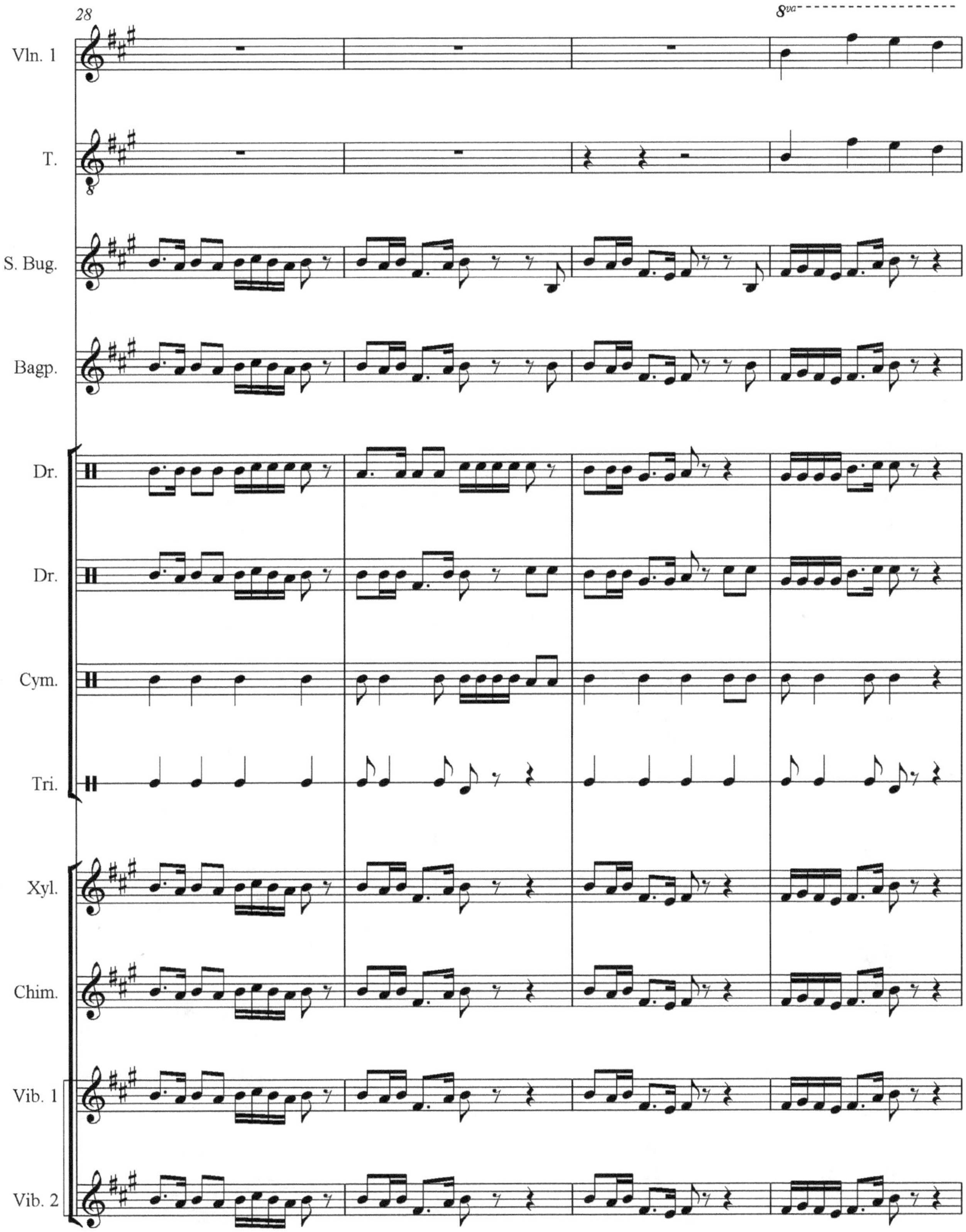
28
8va
Vln. 1
T.
S. Bug.
Bagp.
Dr.
Dr.
Cym.
Tri.
Xyl.
Chim.
Vib. 1
Vib. 2

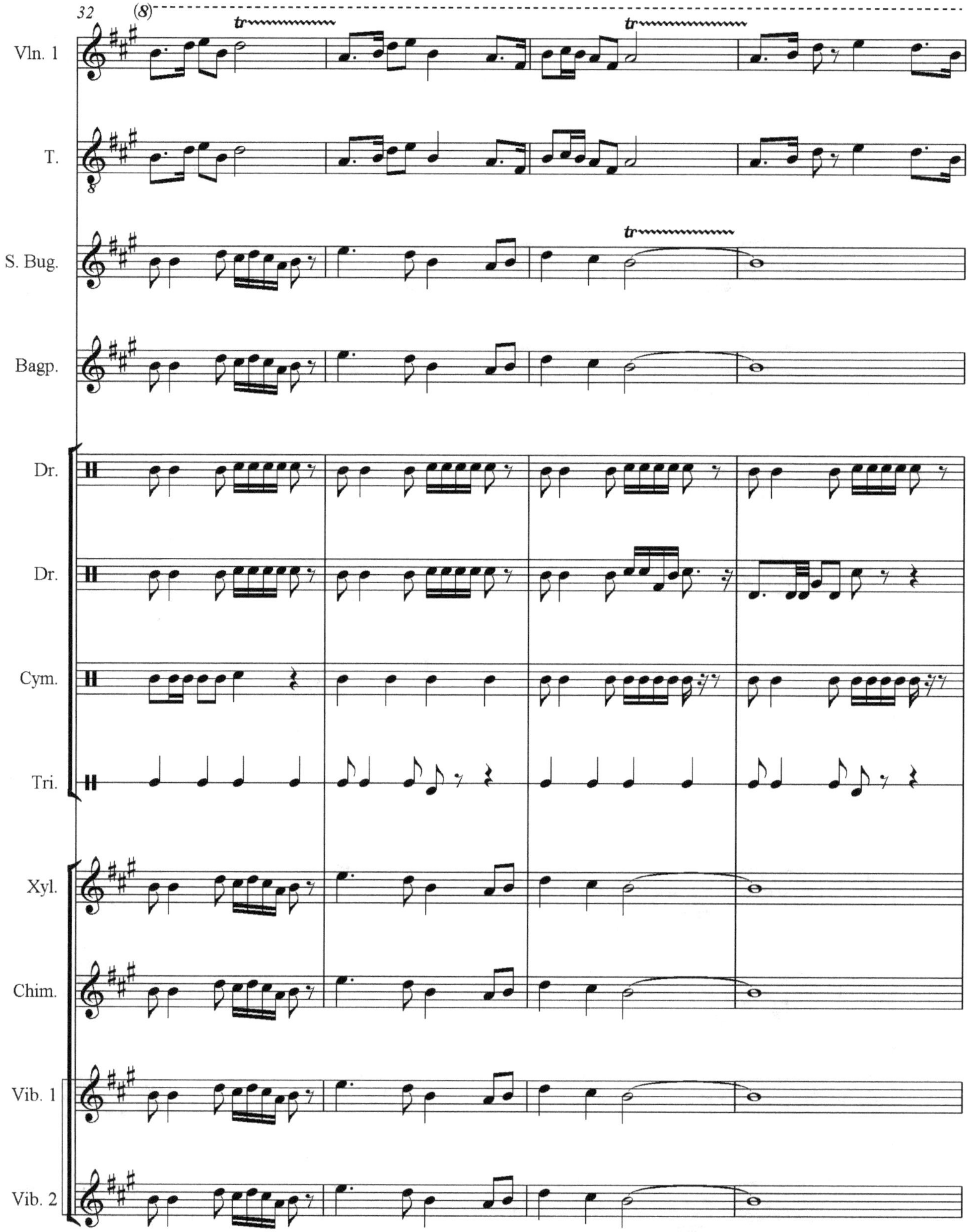
32
(8)
tr
tr
tr
Vln. 1
T.
S. Bug.
Bagp.
Dr.
Dr.
Cym.
Tri.
Xyl.
Chim.
Vib. 1
Vib. 2

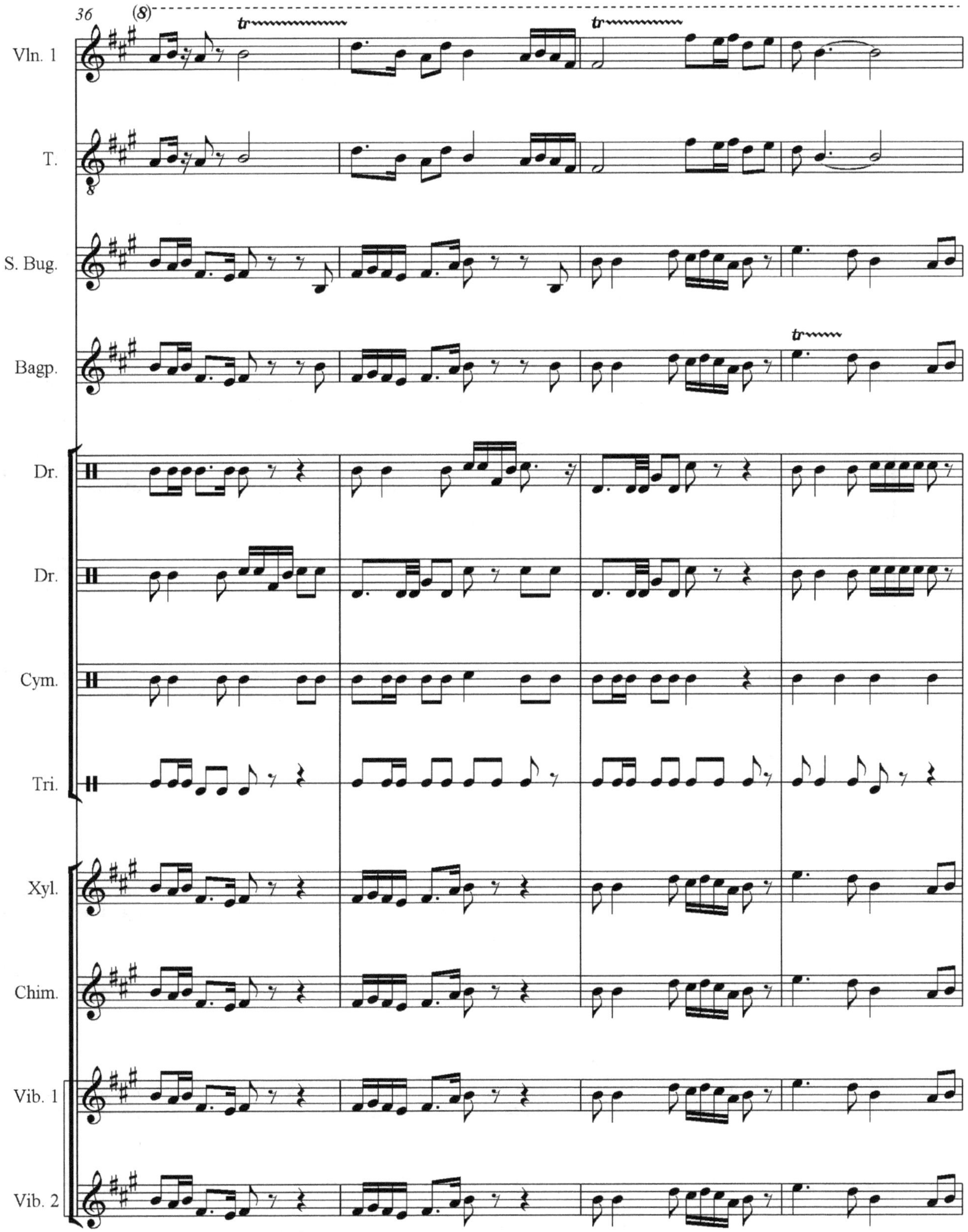
36
(8)
tr
Vln. 1
T.
S. Bug.
Bagp.
Dr.
Dr.
Cym.
Tri.
Xyl.
Chim.
Vib. 1
Vib. 2

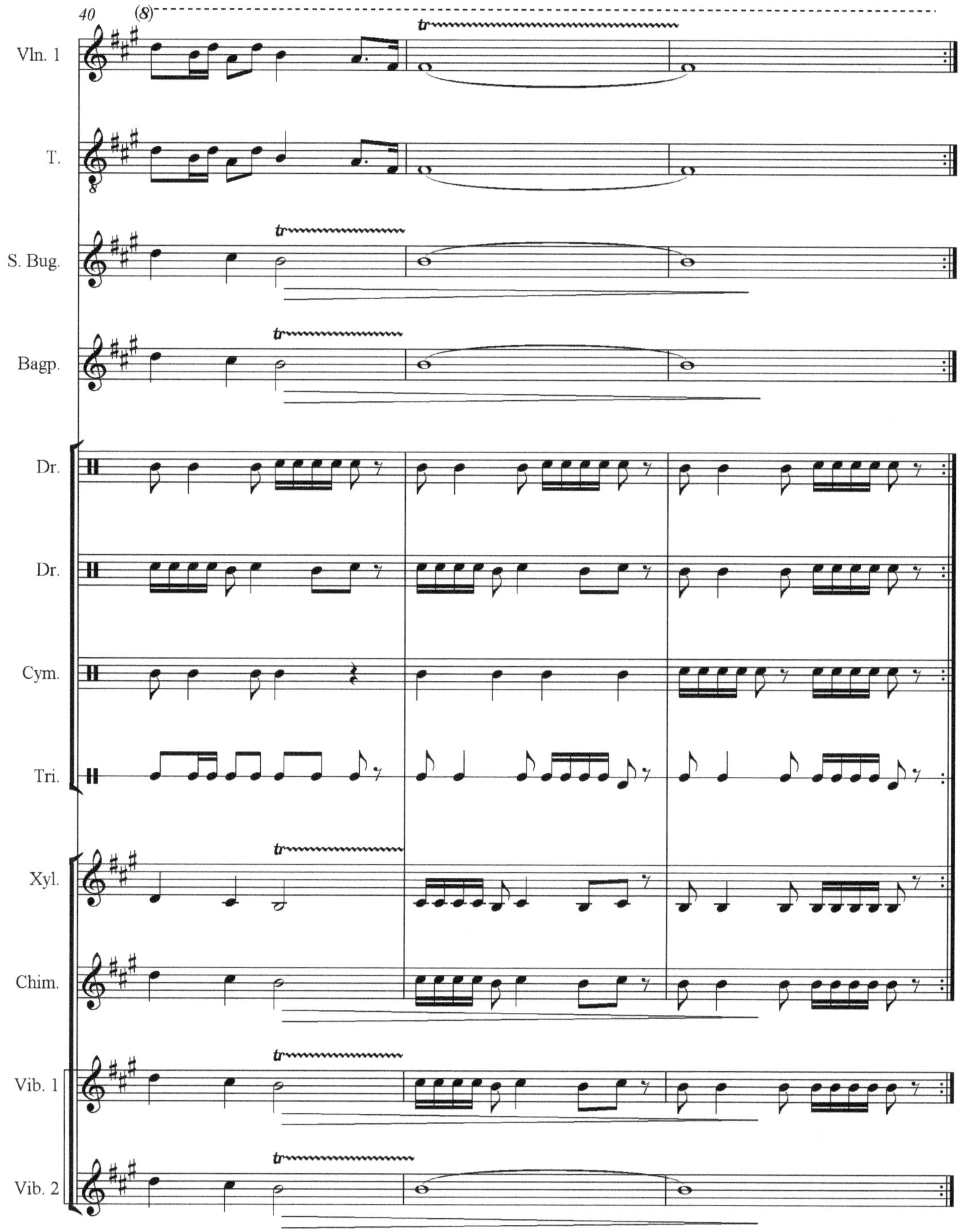
40
(8)
tr
Vln. 1
T.
S. Bug.
Bagp.
Dr.
Dr.
Cym.
Tri.
Xyl.
Chim.
Vib. 1
Vib. 2

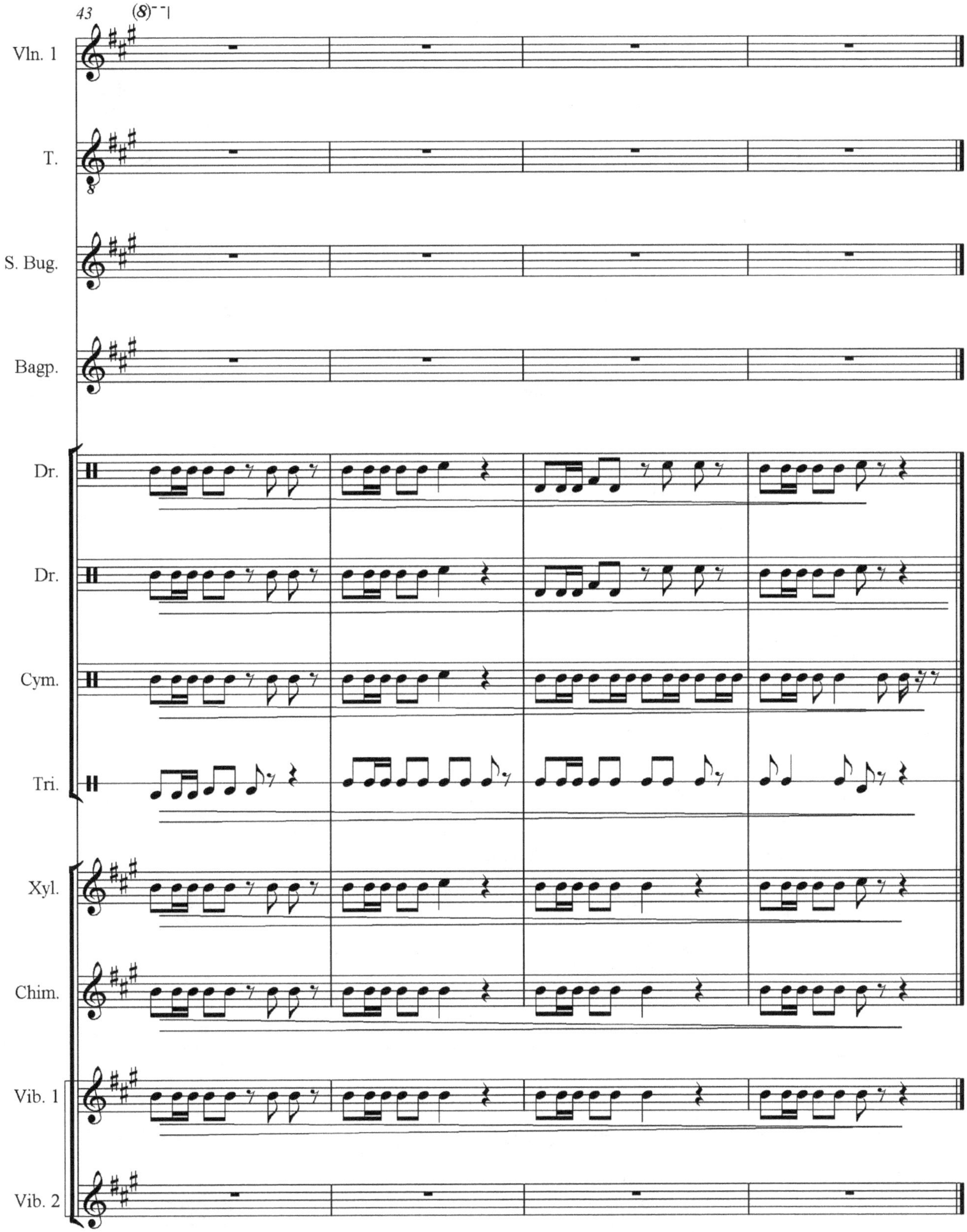

43
(8)
Vln. 1
T.
S. Bug.
Bagp.
Dr.
Dr.
Cym.
Tri.
Xyl.
Chim.
Vib. 1
Vib. 2

Bon Voyage! Olympic Games' Athletes!

Johnson Gao

Johnson Gao

The day___ in the a - re - na, it seemed that

we were real enemies. Ah!_____ But, we say no.___ The

The Human voice for lyrics is the as the voice of violin but no over (8).

2

Lyrics (Vln. 1, m.12): day___ at the end of track, we had_ fought for every inch of field. -

Lyrics (Vln. 1, m.18): - Ah! - - Now we give valu - able gifts to each o - thers. (The) Ah!___

The Human voice for lyrics is the as the voice of violin but no over (8).

114

3

Vln. 1: But, now___ we're good friends.___

Vln. 1: That was due to the force of Olympic Games.___ Let me___ say fare - well

The Human voice for lyrics is the as the voice of violin but no over (8).

4

The Human voice for lyrics is the as the voice of violin but no over (8).

116

About the Lyricist and Musician

Johnson Gao (used name: Kuixiong Gao, listed in the "American Men and Women of Science" for many years), US citizen who was born in Shanghai, China, May 3, 1937. He is a multi-talented "renaissance-type of man". He combines a scientist an artist and a musician in one man.

As a scientist he is a professor of Cell Biology with many research articles and scientific books published, which were related to hormonal interaction, neuroscience, immunohistochemistry, developmental biology and nano-technology (nano-gold drug delivery system). Among those publications one book is very unique: "Polyethylene Glycol as an Embedment for Microscopy and Histochemistry" (edited by Kuixiong Gao and published by CRC Press in 1993; the book is listed at Amazone.com) and he is the editor-in-chief of that book, which is searchable at URL:

http://www.amazon.com/Polyethylene-Glycol-Embedment-Microscopy-Histochemistry/dp/0849343232/ref=si3_rdr_bb_product/103-3717401-1823861

As an artist, he owns a web-based "Gao Gao Gallery", which has more than one hundred pieces of paintings and photos contributed by himself and his two sons. The URL is shown below.

https://finerworks.com/mgallery/artists.asp?U_ID=gaogao

An album of those arts can be viewed at URL:

http://www.scribd.com/doc/13788/An-album-of-Gao-Gao-Gallery-download-for-free

As a musician, he composed many songs. Performances of those songs electronically were published as two music CDs, which were listed at cdbaby.com:

http://www.cdbaby.com/cd/johnsongao http://www.cdbaby.com/cd/johnsongao2

Some of them can be downloaded for free at download.com by searching artist's name Johnson Gao. Among them, two children's songs "For Mammy" and "For Daddy" had got worldwide popularity on the web.

This book is especially for the CD at: http://www.lulu.com/content/2071273.

Johnson Gao had composed several songs electronically during September and October 2007. He had hoped to use those songs to support the coming Olympic Games in Beijing 2008. He submitted four songs with four CDs and 13 copies of music sheets for each song to the Beijing Music Radio according the rules of the Olympic theme song competition instructed. But, he did not receive any acknowledgment of receiving those stuffs from BMR. Then, he wrote several e-mails to them to inquire about the status, but the e-mail address they provided was invalid and no any responses neither. So, he thought that those things had lost in mail and he decided to publish those music pieces by himself. A CD called as "Gao's Music for Olympic Games" was published few days ago. Tracks: 1. Olympic Marching Song. 2. Song for Success. 3. Olympic is Good. 4. Beijing Opera Style Olympic Song. 5. Raise the Championship Cup (version A). 6. Become A Peace Locomotor. 7. Raise the Championship Cup (Version B with Cannon). 8. The Endless Joy (For Lion Dance). Then, he is preparing to publish this music sheet book for that CD and he added few other songs' music sheets into it (refer to another CD "For Love, For Snow & For Echo"). The total page number is now more than one hundred.

The front cover had used an image of an oil-on-canvas painting called "A Ballet Dancer in a Garden" by Raymond Gao in 2008, with special permission.

A sample of Johnson Gao's art painted in 1961 shown at Gao Gao Gallery

https://finerworks.com/mgallery/artists.asp?U_ID=gaogao&offset=12

Errata

Due to the technical complexity in correcting typewrite errors in lyrics and musical note in lines, which were in the format of graphic-type of music sheets and all sheets had been embodied as a huge file of text, I would rather use an errata sheet to correct them, which is a separate short file and could be easily changed in the future when new errors might be found. The following places are errors that have to be corrected by readers.

1. Page28, section 28, Tenor's music notes, "DF#D" should be changed to "DED".

2. Page53, section 36, Choir, lyrics, "clibing" should be changed to "climbing".

3. Back cover line 6, word 6 "peace" should be changed to "Peace".

4. Page 2, Soprano, lyrics, English used "Olympic" as a noun. It can be replaced with another word "Olympiad". There are some other places like that in this book. Readers may change them as they like.

B